POETRY TO SURVIVE DEPRESSION

Gregory Mcilwaine

Kindle

ISBN-13: 9798569055555

Cover design by: Art Painter
Library of Congress Control Number: 2018675309
Printed in the United States of America

Introduction

Hi everyone, Firstly, thank you for choosing my book. My name is Gregory Mcilwaine and I live in a place called Craigavon, in Co. Armagh, Northern Ireland. Throughout my life I have worked in a wide variety of roles such as chef, youth worker, support worker in a homeless hostel, factory worker, security officer and self-defence instructor.

Six years ago that all came to an end as from 2002 I started to suffer badly from severe depression and other symptoms of anxiety. These steadily got worse until in 2014 I was diagnosed with Chronic Post traumatic Stress Disorder,(PTSD) due to personal trauma brought on by events throughout my life.

I had started writing poems in my late teens but it wasn't until I became ill and got involved in a creative writing class that I took my poetry seriously and I couldn't get over how my poetry or just writing my feelings down was so therapeutic and had a calming effect and relieved me of some stress as I spilled my heart out on to paper. You don't have to be a poet or any type of expert to write something down in whatever style you prefer.

No one truly knows what it is like to suffer mental illness unless they experience it themselves. I hope I can help you to understand as I describe what it is like to suffer from PTSD and the depression it brings, as best as I can.

I'm publishing this anthology to maybe encourage someone who are suffering similar mental health issues to start writing as a therapy, whether it be poetry, storytelling or just jotting down feelings. Hopefully, through writing, you will find peace and also help others in their struggles. The main thing is that you enjoy it and get some of your worries out of your system. It also works as a distraction from everyday life as you focus on what you are writing.

So I will leave you now with a thought from a few years ago when I was on a creative writing class, someone asked me " Why do you put all your feelings and problems down on paper?" and my response was " Because they are easier to carry that way".

CONTENTS

1. NORN IRON

Well.. What about ye ?,
Let's settle this once and for all.
Ulster is for everyone,
Just as much Billy's as Sean Paul's.

Our wee country is fantastic,
But it's had its ups and downs.
We can't help there is terrorists,
And the country's run by clowns.

Most of the old streets are gone now,
It's all new buildings, Big and bold.
But because of the problems we have had,
The new ones didn't stand as long as the old.

But that's because of the odd bomb,
You used to get them here and there.
It's so sad for those who worked to survive,
As their business went up in the air.

Our countryside and coast is lovely,
And most of the people are 'dead on',
Here in Norn Iron we've some craic,
'Cause it's Guinness and fry's we're fed on.

Well to all you tourists out there,
It's only the bad news you see on T.V.
C'mon and take a wee dander,
You'll love it, wait till ye see.

We'll here's a wee warning for ye,
Just watch what football top ye wear.
Watch what pub ye all go into,

When ye go out on the tear.

C'mon here till I tell ye,
I just go where I'm tuck.
'Cause when it comes to religion,
I don't give a..... damn, Good luck.

2. RUNAWAY TRAIN

Eyes glistened as they looked at the Christmas tree,
The aroma of cinnamon was all around me.
Getting excited about what will be brought,
We hadn't much money, so nothing was sought.

As the big day came nearer, I started to sing,
Jingle bells, jingle bells, was all you could hear ring.
My mind was working overtime, trying to guess,
What will Santa bring, my nerves were in a mess.

I knew my gifts, would be all mum could afford,
She gave us her all, and left the rest to the Lord.
We all got new jammies to wear on Christmas eve,
As we sat watching the annual films of make believe.

When the big night came, we went to bed early,
A nice warm bath with damp ginger hair so curly.
Finding it hard to sleep, with excitement you know,
Staring out of my window, at the moonlit glow.

Gently woke up by my wee mummy, my loving peer,
Whispering wake up, wake up, Santa's been here.
I clambered down the stairs, crashing thru the door,
And wrapped and tagged pressies covered the floor.

He had left a massive railway set, With 21 trains,
I ripped it open as I tossed the torn paper remains.
We were all so happy with what we had got,
For all that we had, we had got quite a lot.

After a lovely dinner and a sing song together,
We were all exhausted, huddled like birds of a feather.
Woke again on Boxing Day, and couldn't wait to play,

But when I got downstairs, my wee heart did decay.

My train set was gone and the other pressies were away,
Distraught with this, as trickling tears were on display.
The Grinch had been up to his same old antics again,
He had sold, drunk and gambled my wee set of trains.

3. TUNNEL OF LIGHT

As she stares out of the window,
In a dreamy state of mind.
Blanking out the hustle and bustle.
Of passengers beside and behind.
Background sound can hardly be heard,
As her blankness tries to fade it out.
She might be constantly staring,
But seeing nothing that's about.
As she daydreams and evaluates,
Life's path and which way to go.
Which way will take her out,
Of her terminal that has no glow.
But as the train enters the tunnel,
She looks deep into her dark past.
She doesn't think of normal good times,
But the bad things forever will last.
As the train departs from the tunnel,
To a whole new world of shining light.
She hopes and dreams of a better day,
And the track of life she chooses is right.

4. QUILT OF COMFORT

As she huddled in under her duvet.
And pulled it up till it reached her eyes.
Whilst the wind blew withered branches,
Scraping the window from outside.
Scared of all the noises around her,
With nostrils filled with the smell of damp.
Lying shivering with the wintery coldness,
And the only light being a candlelit lamp.
The wind was howling like a werewolf,
Down her spine was a shivering streak.
Pestered by the constant dripping noise,
Of a metal pot that was catching a leak.
The doors were slapping against their frames,
With the draughts entering from outside.
She kept thinking someone else was there,
Too afraid to peek as she was so terrified.
Battling with all of her emotions and fears,
With no one around to help her fight.
Her heart racing like a freight train,
And her chest pains of anxiety felt so tight.
As the storm slowly began to calm down,
Her eyes slowly closing unable to stay awake.
Now there was an eerie silence in the room,
As the weather was taking a well-earned break.
The next morning the sun started to shine,
Promises of hope for a bright and wonderful day.
And she knelt by her bedside to say prayers,
Asking god to please take her nightmares away.

5.FROM PILLS TO SKILLS

They say what doesn't kill you makes you stronger,
And for now the deep dark side of me is no longer.
Since David passed away I felt so angry and down,
Smiles were absent being replaced by painful frowns.
On most days I just wanted to sleep them all away,
Just to get thru the darkness and heartfelt decay.
I didn't want to face the everyday things in my life,
Just felt withdrawn in a duvet of sadness and strife.
Not wanting to face or talk to anyone or do anything,
Thinking that depression was all my day would bring.
And then to top it all off, I couldn't pay the hill of bills,
My day constantly consisted of red letters and pills.
If ever go outside you put on the false faced happy mask,
The thoughts of meeting anyone is a sickening task.
But the more you do it and work your triggers out,
And you learn that money isn't what it's all about.
Your health is more important than this you will find,
And fight against your illness, with your strong mind.
Face your demons head on and rise with all your might,
Use your frustration and fears to fuel your inner fight.
Turn your negatives to positives and turn a new leaf,
Find a coping mechanism or some type of stress relief.
I done this by using all the anger and hate i had inside me,
Thinking what I could do to with my darkened energy.
With all the hatred and evil that created my sadness,
I was like a caged animal, about to unleash
all my badness.
So I decided to use my emotions to put it to good use,
And took up martial arts and on a punchbag I let loose.
Whilst working one day, A customer entered the store,

A martial arts hoodie stood out to
me, the one that he wore.
I stopped and asked him, "Do you
know where I could train,
So he said he would ring me and took
my number and name.
And he kept his promise and gave me call in January 2012,
And we got on like a house on fire, I'm glad it went well.
He showed me his perfected system of self-defence skills,
And it wasn't long till I forgot about the Pills and the bills.
Helping me mentally and physically
in any way that it could,
Making my wellbeing and mindfulness making
me feel good.
It was a good distraction from the everyday
darkness I hated,
And my demons and frustrated moods
where slowly sedated.
It gave me confidence and strength
to build my self-esteem,
Turning my reoccurring evil night terrors
into hopeful dreams.
I have earned instructors diplomas
and I'm on an orange belt,
Giving me a boost of pride and joy the
best that I have ever felt.
But I have to say thanks to other things
that gave tranquillity,
Like talking to the wave centre and positive
people surrounding me.
Most important of all my wife Grainne,
her loyalty to me was true,
Enduring my moods and silence every
day and getting me through.
Words of wisdom did help that I would
daily read or write down,

Like beautiful roses grow from thorned
stems and rough grounds.
And regarding my fighting, there's no gain without pain,
Just remember there can't be a rainbow without any rain.

6. TIME TO LOVE

Hello sweetheart, how are keeping you today,
I miss you more and more, every time I am away.
What have you been up to, Anything really nice,
Make sure you live life to the full, That's my advice
I haven't been up to much, What an exciting life.
I just look forward to the day, you become my Wife.
You always look so wonderful, Not a fault in sight,
I always dream about you and us, every single night.
When we do meet we don't get any privacy for us,
People standing staring, what's with all the fuss.
I feel I am the luckiest man, in the entire world,
To have the chance to be with the most beautiful Girl.
I am thankful for every second, That I spend with you,
If you weren't in my life, I wouldn't know what I'd do.
You are so faithful and loyal, you have proven that,
I know I am no angel, Sometimes I can be a twat.
But you have stood by me, Thru thick and thin,
To praise all your good points, where do I begin.
I can't wait to lift your veil, and kiss those red lips,
And honeymoon on a cruise, on one of those big ships.
I yearn for the day when we hear our wedding bells,
But that all depends if I get released from this cell.

7. THE CLINK OF BLING

I was given this item of bling by a well-
groomed gentleman,
Clean shaven and in a lovely suit, with a glowing
golden tan.
Once I put on this bling, my mates all scream and shout,
I am always the talk of the town, I'm all they take about.
My jewellery glistens as the sun shines
thru my window pane,
It's even got a stamp on it from a certain
well established name.
Not everyone can afford to wear it as
it gets everyone's attention,
But the odd celeb has worn it, their
names I refrain to mention.
When I wear it men hold doors open,
especially just for me.
Buzzing me into my apartment, Keeping
me safe with security.
They always look after me and escort
me wherever I choose to go,
I'm always in the camera's eye, in local
newspapers I'm on show.
My bling always matches my outfit, I
think I'm setting a trend,
Most of the time our outfits clash as
they fight to be my friend.
I must say anything I wear makes me
stand out in the crowed,
But then again, I often do things which
are usually not allowed.

And because of this I am where I am in
my life wherever I locate.
That's why my bling is a set of handcuffs issued
by Florida State.

8. THE HOST OF A GHOST

There are not too many that admit to having a Ghost,
There should be more info and help for being the host.
The Ghost that haunts me comes with no invitation,
Without any idea of his unpredictable duration.
It can come and go whenever he likes to do so,
But from that very instant, you want it to go.
It drains your energy with the heaviness that it brings,
Grounding you like a bird of freedom with broken wings.
You cannot see it but it is most definitely there,
I am the only one who can feel its presence to be fair.
It could make you feel so alone in a crowded room,
And turn a house full of fun into a dark Den of gloom.
It takes you from standing rigid as a well-built tower
To shrugging and slouched like a withered
wilting Flower.
From an outgoing and friendly fun-loving
Woman or Man.
Making me withdrawn and unsociable as much as it can.
Others will tell or advise you how to
make the ghost go away
How can I when I can't think as my rationality does decay.
The side effects make me irritated and sick to the gills,
I wish I could turn a can of kickass into ghost killing pills.
I know that only I can fight this battle that haunts me.
It's easier said than done, but that's the way it's got to be.
The problem is that it hits harder than
any other force I know,
And you can't be prepared when it eventually
comes toe to toe.
I will let you in on a secret as the beast inside

me faces a bout.
The ghost is called Depression and I
am going to knock him out.

9. PAPER AND CHALK

During Autumn season in school,
Teacher would bring us on a trail,
My classmates and I would jump
With excitement without fail.
We went on a long educational walk,
To the nearest gardens and park.
We went here to study nature,
But ended up just acting a lark.
Shuffling our feet thru leaves,
Kicking them all over the place,
Wrapped up in Parka Coats
That kept the wind from your face.
Shielding you from the wind
By the fur trimmed funnel type hood,
It was as if you were hiding inside,
And nobody else could see you.
The Boys would try to climb the trees,
To see who could get e highest,
And we would all play hunts and kissy catch,
Except for the shyest.
Some of the boys played soldiers,
Making vocal machine gun rattles,
Mucked up to their eyeballs,
Like someone just home from a battle.
The girls would skip about playing ring-a-rosies,
Around the big oak tree,
Some peeking over at their favourite boy,
Giving out a little tee-hee.
The Teacher would try their hardest,
To keep us all settled down,

But we had other ideas,
Like messing about and acting the clown.
But as we got our study heads on
and calmed to learn something new,
The teacher told us how to tell the age of a tree
and how high it grew.
But what we loved the most,
when we were on our adventurous walk.
Was taking leaf and tree impressions,
with paper and a piece of chalk.

10. LIFE ON THE HIGH STREET

I wake up to the hustle and bustle
of commuters in their flocks,
With people rushing to their work
Like horses out of the blocks.
Men in dapper suits and overcoats,
With newspapers under their arm,
Women in fashionable dresses
and bracelets heavy with gold charms.
As they go by me in a frenzy
like a human tsunami type wave,
I get a whiff of their odours
of their perfume and aftershaves.
The odd one gets dropped off
in their limos outside designer shops,
The bank machines so busy,
the sound of paper notes never stops.
All I hear is the frantic voices
on phone calls about work and shares,
Not having time for anyone else,
Not even recognising they're there.
Blinded by their wealth in their Gucci
sunglasses to stop the rays.
Wrapped up in their clothes
that are made in sweat shops every day.
But what I notice the most of all,
is their footwear and funny socks,
I think, do I want to be their shoes,
While I lie here homeless in my wooden box.

11. STIRRER IN A STEW

The wooden spoon is a treasured utensil,
And just as important as the poets pencil.
It's like Irelands most precious Holy Grail,
Its results will surely please you without fail.
What it conjures up, Will blow your mind,
Your needs will be fulfilled, you will find.
The end result will taste no less than first class,
Warms you up at night, After Church or Mass.
But it's only magical used with other things,
A giant cast iron pot and roasting cooker ring.
My Granny would stir it vigorously, All in a mix,
While Granda stocks the open fire with broken sticks.
Firstly Granny would brown all of the meat,
With all the Grandkids running around her feet.
Then added freshly peeled spuds, and all the veg,
And Granda cut the Nutty Crust as thick as a ledge.
This is a collage of flavours, aromas and tastes,
Fills you up inside and then enlarges your waist.
They say it's best leaving it till the second day,
While hovering over it repeatedly , Like it's your prey.
Taking a sneaky spoonful of it when nobody's around,
As you sniff the meaty scent, like you are a hound.
Yes, it's our tongue tantalizing bowl of Irish Stew,
It's the best meal in the world, take our word, It's true.
We pray before it to say thanks for what were to eat,
As it's dished out to all of us as we sit still in our seats.
It does taste like it has been sent
down from heaven above,
Created perfect with heart & soul,
and seasoned with love.

12. MY IMPRESSION
OF DEPRESSION

Stripped of my freedom for something
I did not create or do,
Wanting to do and see so much and I
have so much time in lieu.
Left in total darkness, looks like I will
never see the light of day,
Getting frustrated is a daily chore, As
my hopes and dreams decay.
The system grounding me and taking control
of all my actions,
Closing all routes I want to venture,
As now I'm truly sectioned.
Will I ever get out of here, as dark and dismal
images enter my head,
As I sit every night worrying about the nightmares
when I'm in my bed.
With the amount of extreme violence and
how real these terrors can be,
Have me shaking inside and out with
cold sweats to a crazy degree.
So involved in the nightmare and knowing
right well that I'm asleep,
Pleading with those involved in it, let
me wake before I fall too deep.
Being totally irritated, yearning to wake
out of this doom and gloom,
Just to feel the safeness and calm again, it
could never happen too soon.

I wake up drained and tired, more than
when I put my head down,
Instead of being ready for a new day, I
feel down as I don a frown.
Even if this place was full of people, I
would feel lonely and insecure,
As the darkness and anxiety trail me down,
like a fish trapped by a lure.
The situation takes away my dignity, and hygiene
is at an all-time low,
As I have nothing to look good for, and nowhere
exciting to ever go.
Getting washed, shaved, and dressed
seems just like a hard day's work,
Even thoughts of facing a store with
crowds send me totally berserk.
Sometimes you can't be bothered eating,
As everything tastes the same,
Just doing it for the hell of it, any decisions
I make feel ever so lame.
I find it hard making the simplest of decisions
when they do arise,
I sit there empty of answers, feeling
dumb as I look up to the skies.
Niggling and annoying as it can turn
out that I usually just give up,
Like you know you're a mug full of tea,
but feel like an empty cup.
I try to keep myself occupied and do all
in my power that I can do,
But I still think I will achieve nothing
as it amounts to feeling blue.
There's not enough advice out there to
stop me getting to this situation,
Lack of resources, info, and guidance,
far too little basic education.

There's no help in between your G.P.
and receiving the right care,
Just left waiting with dangerous thoughts,
with too much time to spare.
Sitting here getting flashbacks, re-enactments
of the trauma I went thru,
And Doctors think that 10 minutes will
be enough to diagnose you.
I'm a test dummy on a production line, Hoping
the tablets will work.
They forget to check your background
and look inside to see what lurks.
Whilst I fight to get to where I want, it's
a sad and meaningless task,
I beg for someone just to listen to me, or
is it that just too much to ask.
By now my memory is down to nothing
and I don't know what day it is,
I can't think rationally and I get all nervous
and my senses are in a fizz.
People could tell you all day long, you
will come out the other end,
But I already know this, it doesn't matter
as it's a fight only I can tend.
I know that people will see me, When I
go for a walk or wherever I be,
And say to others, " I saw him today and
he was looking alright to me".
They don't and can't see the dark demon
that has taken over my inside,
They only see the layer masking me with
a fake smile and pretend pride.
I also have a lack of concentration, Sometimes
I can't even have a chat,
I can't even watch a film because I lose interest
in about 10 minutes flat.

Going through this illness a lack of confidence
is the most common traits,
A Feeling of self-doubt and insecurity and
a massive amount of self-hate.
I hope my story helps you in some way or
helps someone to understand,
And that others like me will get the care
that we thrive for and demand.
And open people's eyes who are blind by
the stigma It's a kind of lunacy,
And explain that we are not just insane
and lepers of an ignorant society.
I know this poem is bunged with information
I hope I got it down to a tee,
But all I yearn for is so plain and simple....
someday I just want to be me.

13. ALL THE LITTLE THINGS

All the little simple things that make you feel good in life,
Make you forget the bad and sweep you away from strife.
Like the strong smell of burning turf
on a cold winters day,
Or the feel of a hot mouthful of coffee
that heats your inlay.
What about when you lie down in a
lovely comfy bed at night,
After a hard day's work sometimes it
feels like a battle or fight.
Then there's being in your jammies
all snug as a bug in a rug,
The best feeling in the world is being inside
someone's hug.
Even getting a text or a call from an old
friend that you haven't seen,
To talk over old stories and catch up
on where you have been.
There's nothing better than seeing an old person
smile with glee,
That tries to communicate by talking
but it causes difficulty.
It's great suddenly getting a whiff and smelling
your favourite smell
It can really turn your feeling inside to
warm and heavenly from hell.
Or even things that remind you of things
that happened years ago,
Things your granny said takes you

high from a lingering low.
What a feeling it is when your alarm
wakes you, an hour before time,
As you knock it off, turn round and doze
off again, oh it is sublime.
So happy to see an old man being
awarded for fighting in a war.
Or seeing a mother get flowers just
for doing her daily chores.
To see a child playing and so cheerful
with their make pretend toy,
The biggest toy gun made from old wood
makes a very happy boy.
One of the nicest things too is the melting
of chocolate in your mouth,
Puts a gigantic smile on your face but
a few inches on down south.
Getting your hair done if you're a lady
or even a new pair of shoes,
Sometimes even a nice warm bubble
bath will take away the blues.
People say it's beautiful to watch a baby
being born so cute and quaint,
Even though it has made some of the hardest
and big men faint.
So it just goes to prove that happiness
isn't about materialistic things,
And that it only takes the littlest of things
that makes one's heart sing.

14. GREGS CLOTHES PEGS

Sitting here chillaxing and thinking
of the good old times,
When life was wonderful and there
weren't so many crimes.
Remember how you used to have a Budgie or BMX Bike,
Or maybe a Bomber or Chopper, they
were as cool as u like.
And to be cooler, you used to try to get the loudest sound,
And attached a clothes peg and piece of
card that was lying around.
Clipping it unto the frame at the back
wheel, we thot we were cool,
And go as fast as we can, head pushing forward,
like a raging bull.
Listening for that flapping noise to make
a sound like a motorbike,
Riding around the streets in our black
P.E. plimsolls, defo not Nikes.
I remember the guns we use to sit and
make with our own bare hands,
Made out of a piece of wood, a clothes peg
and a bunch of elastic bands.
I would get a long stick, oblong and about
2 feet long and test it out,
I would tuck it into the crease of my shoulder,
In my sniper hideout,
I would close one eye and imagine I was looking
down the sights,
Once it's made, we would have war
games and pretend army fights.

So now I would get my clothes peg and attach
it to the top of my gun,
Joining elastics stringing them together
and load it ready for some fun.
That's what we did to take up our time,
way back in days of old,
When we had respect for our parents
and done what we were told.

15. I WISH

This poem is for all the special little Children,
Living underneath this Earths dome,
I wish I had a giant estate of Houses,
To give each and every one a home.
I wish I could make a clone of myself,
When it's time for them to play,
And I wish I had enough Medicine,
To make all their ailments decay.
I wish I had the longest arms,
So I could hug them all together,
I wish I had the biggest Camera,
To snapshot their smiles and keep forever.
I wish I had all the toys in the world,
To keep them laughing, forever on hold,
And I wish to have the biggest heat source,
To give them sunshine when they're cold.
I wish I had the largest shield of Steel,
To protect them from neglect and pain.
I wish I had the biggest umbrella,
To shelter them from any stormy rain.
I wish I had the world's largest hand,
To catch them when they faint or fall.
I wish I had the strongest hearing aid,
To be there for them when they cry or call.
I wish I had an enormous jam jar.
To be able to bottle all their beauty,
It's because of ailments that they have,
That makes them such little cuties.
I wish for this to go out to all the kids,
That battle through syndrome and disease,

I wish I had the biggest soft Blanky,
To give them comfort and feel at ease.
I wish I had a gigantic working machine,
That turns my heart and soul into a cure.
So I could give my life to all these Kids,
And make them happy, healthy, and pure.

16. A WARDEN WITHOUT A WARNING

As he stands over me with an evil grin
on his face while he sniggers,
The more I cry and sadden his grin gets bigger and bigger.
He makes his presence known with a sarcastic
" Enjoy the ride ",
As my heartfelt fears boil inside me
and spill slowly outside.
A gut-wrenching feeling of hopelessness,
that I totally despise,
Good memories turn into tears that
flow from my reddened eyes.
He overlooks and makes sure that I
am far from in control,
I'm yearning as he chuckles, wondering
will I ever get parole.
He does his best to antagonize me, Every now and then,
Never letting me settle or calm, As he repeatedly offends.
He strips me of everything, Right down to the bone,
And all of my dreams of release he makes me postpone.
Nothing here to tell me when my time
here will or will not end,
Nothing to occupy me here, even if
I do sometimes intend.
My surroundings are in darkness,
Edged with a wall of fear,
A place where you can trail your feet
through your own tears.
No contact with the outside world,

Not a chance of escape,
An area of nothingness, With an atmospheric
hell like shape.
You lose all inhibitions, All the dignity,
and self-motivation,
As if your whole inner person has
taken an awful vacation.
From this crime I did not commit, I
could not even abscond,
And because of what it is, you don't get bail or a bond.
The warden pinpoints every nerve ending
that I do possess,
Repeatedly torturing them with a hateful
grinding type of stress.
He chisels deeply into them with all the force that he has,
And lets out a bellowing roar of fulfilment
as he creates crass.
I sit in the corner quivering like a child
in a total diminished state,
Only a person who has gone through
any of this, Is able to relate.
As he bullies me, I wish there was somewhere
I could have hid,
But I am doing everything I can so that
I don't blow off my lid.
He pokes and teases you, till he grinds
you down once again,
As he just thrives to see you suffer with
your extreme inner pain.
I have had time to think about this and
for you, I will try to simplify,
The shortest of explanations to make
you understand, I will try.
The scenario is that I'm in a jail cell that
I don't want for or demand.
As Depression laughs at me crying, with

the keys of my soul in his hand.

17. SNOW TIME TO MOPE

Fluffy bright white soft snowflakes fall,
Crisped up by the cold blue ice.
Floating down through the atmosphere,
Feeling chilly but eye-tastically nice.
Carpeting the hardened damp soil,
With a blanket of glittery flashing.
Capping each branch it falls upon,
Slowly drips as the rain starts lashing.
Dampening and slowly melts the field,
As it lies vacant due to hibernation.
Sleeping livestock huddled up in sheds,
As nature puts a stop to crop creation.
The only noise I can hear is little chirps,
Fr e frequent call of the Robin Redbreast.
As it feeds on the tiny crimson berries,
From the holly bush with plenty to digest.
As I inhale I get this sudden rush of fresh air,
Untouched by the usual farmyard smells.
As I trudge along each footstep crunches,
And disturbs the smooth white winter fell.
Arriving at the brook where I would often fish,
The water trickles as it meanders down.
The feisty trout being nowhere to be seen,
My head shakes in disappointment, As I frown.
Ah well, There's no rest when you're a Farmer,
Back to the grindstone, Not knowing how to cope.
Stuff to be maintained and fixed for next season,
And I have no time to stand here and mope.

18. LIGHT FROM DARK

As the storm blows ferociously in from the east.
Making rolling waves pushed by an enraged beast.
The treacherous storm does not discriminate or care,
Whoever gets in its path will be filled with despair.
They will be crushed and die or be scarred for life,
And never forget this era of their hardship and strife.
But there is a beacon of hope that will warn us afore,
Sending out signals telling us to be prepared for a war.
Saving us from crashing into the jagged rock shore,
Or the rolling towering seas that are in an uproar.
The lighthouse is there to guide us gently through,
Any storms or dark times that we could ensue.
Sometimes we can't see what's actually going on,
We are blinded because our emotions are so strong.
And everything around us is masked by a red mist,
So the lighthouses siren bellows out as it persists.
It will never give up on us or ever refrain to work,
It will always be there wherever danger does lurk.
You can always rely on it to step up to the mark,
And guard you unconditionally from the first spark.
As the storm settles and light emerges from the dark,
The lighthouse stands down to let nature do its part.
But it permanently stands tall at our beck and call,
And we can always rely on it to help anytime we fall.
As the light takes over and a distant rainbow appears,
Our hearts lighten and eradicate any of our worst fears.
So in a time like now, we have to abide when we're
warned,
And stay inside to keep us safeguarded from the storm.
Focussing on our loved ones with all of our utmost care.

Becoming their lighthouse of hope and always be there.

19. PRESENT DAY WAR

Here's a few words to describe me,
I am naturally muscular & perfectly toned.
I have a pair of piercing pale blue eyes,
And a crew cut, no need to be combed.
I am very flexible and fit to be fair,
To help me in any situation you put me in.
The only imperfections that I have,
Are a scarred cheek and a chiselled chin.
But in saying that I'm very lucky indeed,
And to be honest, I'm the best at what I do.
So my handlers sent a letter of request,
Out of hundreds I was handpicked, That's true.
So I have been drafted to my new mission,
Unlucky for me, Tomorrow's Christmas Day.
As soon as I get there, I go undercover,
And not one part of me can be seen on display.
But as the day breaks and the sunlight shines,
My cover is blown and my hideouts a disgrace.
As I get manhandled so roughly by strangers,
Until they see who I am and recognize my face.
They grip me tightly with utter excitement,
Like I'm a hero or a legend in their eyes.
But no time to rest, We're on a mission,
So I changed into my camouflage disguise.
I'm hurled straight into the battlefield,
Mucked up to my eyeballs and some more.
My handler touches the back of my head,
To warn me to keep a good lookout afore.
As my eyes scan the area from side to side,
I spot the enemy and I aim and start to fire.

As the rat-a-tats echo, ringing in my ears,
Enemy falling like dominos into the mire.
The battle is over and now it's time to recoup,
My handler sits me down, to let me rest easy.
As the light of day becomes a cloak of dark,
Our hut sheltering us from the cold and breezy.
So it's time to retire after another crazy day,
The lights go out and my mode is set to stealth.
My bed feels as stiff as a hard wooden board,
And like the elf, I'm sat back up on the shelf.

Happy Christmas From Action Man.

20. PAWS FOR A WHILE

I've had a pet Dog for quite a while, It's always on Toe,
It follows me everywhere, Where ever it tells me to go.
But if I want to go somewhere it's a battle and a half,
It is so strong that it will easily stop me in my path.
It gets jealous of me trying to be sociable or even fun,
Being like a barrier so I can't engage with anyone.
It rules my life most of the time laying down the law,
And if I try to fight it, it hits me with a sweeping paw.
It sits and watches over me while I sleep in my bed,
While I have night Terrors that are at war inside my head.
I wake the next morning more tired than before I slept,
Deciding what to do today and it is never of any help.
It isolates me from meeting up with people I rarely see,
I feel no one wants to be lumbered by my Dog and me.
As it snaps at those around you for no good reason at all,
Making my anxiety rise rapidly as my
patience quickly falls.
It's never that well behaved it would
really sink your soul,
Getting great enjoyment, Drinking
your tears from its bowl.
I beg for it to go away and I won't
have to face it ever again,
I won't have it accompanying me and my anxiety
will refrain.
Someday hopefully I can tame it when
I will be in command,
And it will leave me alone and I will have the upper hand.
I can't wait till the day our friendship
will go out of fashion,

And I will get rid of my Dog whose name is depression.

21. TIDES OF TEARS

It was a frosty cold and stormy winters night,
And the only thing that stood out in our sights.
Was the torrential rain highlighted as it pours,
By the Lighthouses luminated ray on the shore.
The wind howled and whistled a gale of cold,
Waves smashed against rocks as they rolled.
The siren roared deep sounded warning to ships,
Just in case the light was hidden by thick foggy mist.
We could hear the row of docked boats knock,
And their bells peel as they swayed and rocked.
I don't know how the birds stay up in that sky,
Getting battered by the gusts from every side.
But our main focus was on the distant seas,
As our men were out trawling against our pleas.
We warned them not to, But it's in their blood.
They are only happy when they're battling floods.
There's no other work they would want to do,
And unemployment is high on this wee island too.
We hope they are homeward bound and afloat,
And make a return in that monstrosity of a boat.
I feel sick in the stomach from worry and nerves,
That they will fight thru what the sea gods serve.
We decide to call it a day with our hopes depleted,
Hoping that today's outcome won't be repeated.
Wishing tomorrow has clearer skies and calm seas,
And maybe a joyous result that will set us at ease.
I hardly slept a wink all night thinking of my man,
And all the worst scenarios thru my mind they ran.
As the sun slowly peeks out from the horizon afar,
Promising good weather and still waters on par.

But natures aftermath is in total wreck and ruin,
The harbour masters base has took a real doing.
He has no way to contact any of his small fleet,
As the radars mast has been badly bruised and beat.
So all we can rely on is our hopes and prayers,
So God guides them into the sights of binoculars.
We all look on eagerly squinting with the glimmer,
As the sun reflects off the ripples as they shimmer.
We look to the heavens above and decide to pray,
That we get to witness the return of our men today.
Holding each other in a bond of unity thru hope,
And the trawler appears gradually into our scope.
As forced smiles sneak thru our quivering lips,
Relieved sort of, but taking nothing for granted yet .
As it gets closer, we see silhouetted figures emerge.
The suspense is imminent as we are still on the verge.
The boat carefully docks as we all let out a cheer.
As the crew throws the rope to be attached to the pier.
And one by one the eager men slowly disembark.
Tired and soaked thru showing mariners trademarks.
The families and friends run towards them to reunite
Holding them close with a bonding grip so tight.
Hugging them as if they had been away for years,
Emotions spilled out in a torrent of joyous tears.
As they held their loved ones face as their lips meet.
Every moment of worry was worth
it as yearning depletes.
The crowds entwined in a heartfelt loving embrace,
As a tear peeks out and trickles down my reddened face.
As I receive the sad news that my man was sadly took,
By the treacherous seas as the trawler
boat violently shook.
I cried tides of tears and my heart sunk like a shipwreck,
With my head in my hands I slouch down and reflect
My man had been crushed just like the dreams of my life,
As tomorrow I was supposed to become

my man's good wife.

22. POST BREAKDOWN

Just into work to be given the sack,
The boss just told me, where to go to.
Pack yer bags and get out of here,
And close that gate behind you.
I drove round for hours and hours,
And went for walks 6 days a week.
Knocking on neighbours doors
From netted curtains they take a peek.
I would wake up early most mornings.
And throw on the same outfit as the day before
As I pass folk jogging or walking their pets
Dogs barking at me as their daily chore.
But I still get ready and go out,
No matter if it rains, hails or snows.
At least in the summer I can wear my shorts
No matter what weather, I have the clothes.
Of course as soon as I get dressed
My hands hug a hot cup of Yorkshire tea.
And I have daily bowl of ready break
With a smidgen of sweet honey.
I must say I do look forward of a morning
to receive parcels and some post
But receiving bills in brown envelopes
is what I truly detest the most.
But it's not all doom or gloom
And things aren't as they seem
Because this is the story of my life
As a postman on my daily routine.

23. WHAT ON EARTH

As I was watching an old man doing his gardening one day,
Digging with such anger, he was surely making
the ground pay.
It made me think that how tending to
the earth can be like life,
The undergrowth and olden ground symbolizing
hurt and strife,
No matter how many times, you turn
it over again and again,
It never goes away and it's hard to
cover up or decay the pain.
And if you throw new soil on it just to
make it look okay or good,
The old memories are preyed upon
and used as nature's food.
The new soil that covers it up is just
there as an optical illusion,
Because what's underneath is ground
in, and a false delusion.
Other people will dig up that ground
again not helping at all,
It only makes the old dirt fresh and
gives the feelings a recall.
So sometimes it's better to tend it on
your own, to get the job done,
Only you feel the real hurt and have a
heart like a dark soiled stone.
But if you think about it when you are studying
your life as ground,
There cannot be a wonderful flower bed without

some dirt around.
So as all things are meant to be and
going according to plan,
Do I sit and watch it rot away or make it beautiful
and take a stand.
You take it slowly, as the flowering process
takes some precious time,
First, you plant happy seeds that will
bloom and make you feel sublime.
It won't happen straight away and you
need to learn as you go,
Just remember not to plant bad seeds as
you will reap what you sew.
Stay away from watering with the wrong liquids,
As they will not gain,
They will just make you rot some more
and only prolong the pain.
So turn your bad soil into a budding beautiful
flowering garden,
And all the hard work you put in will pay
off and make you hardened.
This also can be helped if your friends
and family tend to help you,
When you're feeling stuck in the mud or
just feeling in a mood of blue.
So because you planted all these seeds,
the roots will always be there,
And if you ever come up against old soil
again, you will be prepared.
So as you stand proud looking at the way
the garden has gone to plan.
You have toiled through the dirt and prevailed,
with your own two hands.

24. CARP DIEM

As I went to the lake to fish for a few hours
I smelt the freshly cut grass and blooming flowers.
Listening to the chirps of the myriad of birds
And moos of the cows going about in their herds.
And watching to see if there was movement on the lake,
From the native carp the stillness they would break.
I reach for my rod and bait up my end tackle.
The boilie on the bait screw feeling shackled.
Lifting the tip of my rod, letting off the bail arm,
Till its slightly behind my head ready to cast my charm.
Like a sniper staring down the microscopic sight to aim.
I focus on where it lands as the force of the lead I tame.
I drop the tip of rod and reel in the rest of the slack.
Set the rod on the rest, set alarms ready for attack.
I put on my sunglasses to kill the waters glare.
Whilst watching carp stealthily patrol
from here to there.
I sit patiently while I have drink and a vape,
And bask in natures beauty in this heavenly escape.
Awaiting the sound of the alarms and whizz of the line.
That would definitely make my day complete
and sublime.

25. WOODEN WANT TO LEAVES

One thing I always wanted, Was a giant Sycamore tree,
With an awesome tree hut in it for my mates and me.
It would be the coolest play place, you could ever get,
I could hide in it from the rain and never getting wet.
Perched really high, Hugged by the branches and leaves,
By the time I climbed up to it, I could hardly breathe.
Down below I could see all of the garden and flowers,
And beside me other trees matured bigger than towers.
The branches from each of them reaching
out to each other,
Like they are holding hands to strengthen one another.
It is such a magical place, Filled with my favourite toys,
My own special hideaway envied by
the other girls and boys.
This massive structure made from all old cuts of wood,
Fixed together by rustic nails that
Dad thought were no good.
It had a rickety window covered by
a set of Mummy's Nets,
On the floor a giant beanbag, I loved to sink in its depths.
If you lay back, and looked up, the skylight revealed stars,
Scattered beside it was comics, Sweet
papers and toy cars.
I even decided to cover the floor with
worn carpet and a rug,
Just to make it feel warmer and homely
and a bit more snug.
I put up a wooden sign outside, saying "Do not trespass",
Or you would get catapulted with marbles I had amassed.
I also had a special tin, that concealed

all my treasured things,
Like Action Man, old coins and a winning
conker on a string.
Hidden underneath the carpet was an
emergency escape hatch,
Secured tightly with a brand new
shiny chrome effect latch.
From the roof came a rope that I
could swiftly slide down,
That would take me to a bare part in
the wet grassy ground.
I loved it in the summer when my mates were off school,
Everyone wanted to be my friend,
Which I thought was cool.
We would sit in a circle in the eerie darkness of nights,
Telling one another ghost stories that
made us jump with fright.
But that sums up my den of mischief and make believe,
If I had one of these, surely "I wooden want to leaves".

26. BITTER SWEET BASKING

Sitting in the garden on a beautiful warm sunny day,
Enjoying the heat-wave and soaking up all the rays.
Basking in summer-wear with my sun factor on,
Feeling a slight breeze from mother nature's air-con.
Donning a nice pair of expensive tinted sunglasses,
Smelling the aromas of flowers and freshly cut grasses.
As the bees are buzzing on a mission to find some food,
I recline in my deckchair and feeling in a relaxing mood.
Sipping on bittersweet lemons and sparkling fizz,
With a tongue-tastic taste and a mouthful of bliss.
Reading a good book or gossip from a magazine,
Whilst the washing is on the line smelling so clean.
Listening to the birds as they sing their cheerful song,
It's a form of heaven where scents and senses belong.
Beautiful clouds are formed liked plump pillows of fluff,
All shapes and sizes and soft like the skies powder puffs.
The sun beaming down as I feel the warmth hug my face,
I wouldn't dream of enjoying myself in any other place.

27. WHEN THE GLOVES COME OFF

When the gloves come off.
And the lockdown is lifted.
Social distancing stops
And rules have shifted.
The pandemic phases out
As our trickling tears dissolve
We are still nervously unsure
In what we are forcibly involved.
What can or can't we do now
To keep us out of dangers way
And people aren't listening
To what the professionals say
Society is blind to the evidence
As our population declines.
Family trees bruised and pruned
We console each other and pine.
It's what comes out of this I fear
As mental health is going to rise
One curve being flattened
While another starts to thrive.
People will take one mask off
To put a metaphoric one back on
One that's hidden from onlookers
To camouflage what has gone
Due to isolation and frustration
Spills out downpours of tears
Eventually they will all dry up
And the rainbow of hope will reappear.

28. STAR OF THE SILENT SCREAM

No one can hurt me without my consent
With a protective shell to shield me and prevent
From the predator so he becomes the targeted prey
Giving me the mindset to fight for another day.
But the only person I fear is the one within me
That's scarred and bruised by my mentality.
As I give up on all of my hopes and begging prayers
My beliefs and dreams are diminished as I despair
But I don't have to fight as often as I have had
But still don't have good days just bad and very bad.
I will keep on fighting till I am finally done
And never stop until I get myself back to square one.
As I say goodbye to the pain of the silent scream
And my true self can now be externally seen.

Thank you for reading this book and I hope it inspires, educates or gives you hope.
There is no rainbows without a little rain.

Printed in Great Britain
by Amazon

50888784R00037